STATES

PENNSYLVANIA

A MyReportLinks.com Book

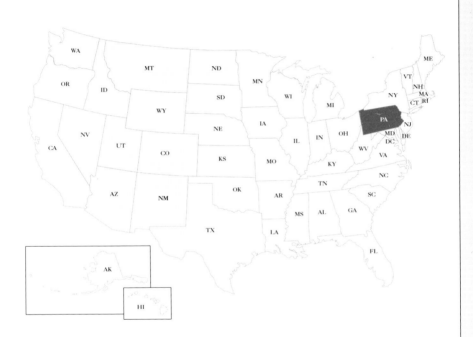

Kim A. O'Connell

MyReportLinks.com Books

an imprint of

 Enslow Publishers, Inc.

Box 398, 40 Industrial Road
Berkeley Heights, NJ 07922
USA

MyReportLinks.com Books, an imprint of Enslow Publishers, Inc. MyReportLinks is a trademark of Enslow Publishers, Inc.

Library of Congress Cataloging-in-Publication Data

O'Connell, Kim A.
  Pennsylvania / Kim A. O'Connell.
    p. cm. — (States)
Summary: Discusses the land and climate, economy, government, and history of the Keystone State. Includes Internet links to Web sites, source documents, and photographs related to Pennsylvania.
Includes bibliographical references (p.   ) and index.
  ISBN 0-7660-5153-6
  1. Pennsylvania—Juvenile literature. [1. Pennsylvania.] I. Title.
II. States (Series : Berkeley Heights, N.J.)
  F149.3.O27 2003
  974.8—dc21
                              2003003672

Printed in the United States of America

10 9 8 7 6 5 4 3 2 1

To Our Readers:
Through the purchase of this book, you and your library gain access to the Report Links that specifically back up this book.

The Publisher will provide access to the Report Links that back up this book and will keep these Report Links up to date on **www.myreportlinks.com** for three years from the book's first publication date.

We have done our best to make sure all Internet addresses in this book were active and appropriate when we went to press. However, the author and the Publisher have no control over, and assume no liability for, the material available on those Internet sites or on other Web sites they may link to.

The usage of the MyReportLinks.com Books Web site is subject to the terms and conditions stated on the Usage Policy Statement on **www.myreportlinks.com**.

A password may be required to access the Report Links that back up this book. The password is found on the bottom of page 4 of this book.

Any comments or suggestions can be sent by e-mail to comments@myreportlinks.com or to the address on the back cover.

Contents

MyReportLinks.com Books
Great Books, Great Links, Great for Research!

MyReportLinks.com Books present the information you need to learn about your report subject. In addition, they show you where to go on the Internet for more information. The pre-evaluated Report Links that back up this book are kept up to date on **www.myreportlinks.com**. With the purchase of a MyReportLinks.com Books title, you and your library gain access to the Report Links that specifically back up that book. The Report Links save hours of research time and link to dozens—even hundreds—of Web sites, source documents, and photos related to your report topic.

Please see "To Our Readers" on the Copyright page for important information about this book, the MyReportLinks.com Books Web site, and the Report Links that back up this book.

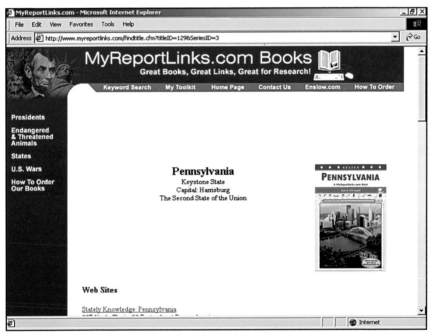

Access:

The Publisher will provide access to the Report Links that back up this book and will try to keep these Report Links up to date on our Web site for three years from the book's first publication date. Please enter **SPA3538** if asked for a password.

Report Links

➤ The Internet sites described below can be accessed at
http://www.myreportlinks.com

*EDITOR'S CHOICE

▶ **Stately Knowledge: Pennsylvania**
On this site from the Internet Public Library, you can learn about the
state of Pennsylvania. The origin of the state's name, points of interest,
and famous people from the state are just some of the things you can
find here.
Link to this Internet site from http://www.myreportlinks.com

*EDITOR'S CHOICE

▶ **U.S. Census Bureau: State and County**
Quick Facts: Pennsylvania
This site from the United States Census Bureau contains facts and
figures relating to the state of Pennsylvania. Here you will find
population, demographic, and housing information; economic
statistics; and more.   Link to this Internet site from http://www.myreportlinks.com

*EDITOR'S CHOICE

▶ **Essays and Information About Hershey History**
This Hershey archives site offers the history of the Hershey Foods
Company and the town of Hershey, Pennsylvania. Here you will find
the story of the chocolate company's founder, among other things.

Link to this Internet site from http://www.myreportlinks.com

*EDITOR'S CHOICE

▶ **PA PowerPort**
Pennsylvania's official government site contains information about
the state's government, geography, economy, history, tourism, and
other topics.

Link to this Internet site from http://www.myreportlinks.com

*EDITOR'S CHOICE

▶ **Explore the States: Pennsylvania**
America's Story, a Library of Congress Web site, contains a number
of short articles about Pennsylvania. Topics include the Civil War in
Pennsylvania, the city of Pittsburgh, National Freedom Day, and more.

Link to this Internet site from http://www.myreportlinks.com

*EDITOR'S CHOICE

▶ **The *World Almanac for Kids Online:* Pennsylvania**
This site contains an overview of vital Pennsylvania state facts. Here
you will find information about land and resources, population,
education and cultural activity, government and politics, economy,
and history.
Link to this Internet site from http://www.myreportlinks.com

Report Links

 The Internet sites described below can be accessed at
http://www.myreportlinks.com

▶**Bethlehem Steel**
Bethlehem Steel was founded in 1904 by Charles Schwab. This site from
Bethlehem, PA Online contains the story of the rise and fall of Bethlehem
Steel and the town of Bethlehem, Pennsylvania.

Link to this Internet site from http://www.myreportlinks.com

▶**The Centennial Exhibition—Philadelphia 1876**
The Centennial Exhibition of 1876, a world's fair, was also the official
one-hundredth birthday party for the United States. This site offers a virtual
tour of the exhibition, which was an important event in Philadelphia's history.

Link to this Internet site from http://www.myreportlinks.com

▶**Doc Heritage**
Doc Heritage, a site of the Pennsylvania State Archives, contains images
and transcriptions of documents important to the state's history as well as
background information on them.

Link to this Internet site from http://www.myreportlinks.com

▶**Documents from the Continental Congress and
the Constitutional Convention**
This Library of Congress site offers original documents, illustrations, and
other resources having to do with America's Continental Congress, which met
in Philadelphia and helped pave the way to independence.

Link to this Internet site from http://www.myreportlinks.com

▶**Fallingwater**
Frank Lloyd Wright is considered one of the most famous American
architects. Many consider his masterpiece to be Fallingwater, in western
Pennsylvania. The official site of Fallingwater includes Wright's biography,
facts about the structure, and visitor information.

Link to this Internet site from http://www.myreportlinks.com

▶**50 States: Pennsylvania**
At this site, you can find information ranging from when Pennsylvania
became a state to what the state song is. Be sure to check out "Fast Facts"
for some interesting trivia.

Link to this Internet site from http://www.myreportlinks.com

Report Links

 The Internet sites described below can be accessed at
http://www.myreportlinks.com

▶ The Gettysburg Address
Following the Battle of Gettysburg, Abraham Lincoln gave one of the
most famous speeches in the history of the United States, the Gettysburg
Address. This Library of Congress Web site contains two drafts of the
speech, Lincoln's invitation to speak at Gettysburg, and more.

Link to this Internet site from http://www.myreportlinks.com

▶ Heinz: About Heinz
The H. J. Heinz Company, with headquarters in Pittsburgh, is
one of the largest food companies in the world. Here you will find
information about the company, its advertising history, and milestones.

Link to this Internet site from http://www.myreportlinks.com

▶ James Buchanan (1857–1861)
This Web site provides a comprehensive biography of James Buchanan,
born in Pennsylvania. Here you will learn about his life, family,
presidency, domestic and foreign policies, and his legacy.

Link to this Internet site from http://www.myreportlinks.com

▶ The Kennedy Center Honors: Bill Cosby
Bill Cosby, the stand-up comedian, movie and television star,
best-selling author, and philanthropist, is also a Pennsylvania
native. Here you will find a brief biography highlighting his
many accomplishments.

Link to this Internet site from http://www.myreportlinks.com

▶ National Constitution Center
On this site from the National Constitution Center, located
in Philadelphia, you can read about the history of the U.S.
Constitution and the people who helped to create it.

Link to this Internet site from http://www.myreportlinks.com

▶ National Park Service: Gettysburg National Military Park
Gettysburg National Military Park is the site of the Battle of
Gettysburg, which marked a turning point in the Civil War.
Here you will find an in-depth history of the battle, visitor
information, and much more.

Link to this Internet site from http://www.myreportlinks.com

Back   Forward   Stop   Review   Home   Explore   Favorites   History

Report Links

 The Internet sites described below can be accessed at
http://www.myreportlinks.com

▶**National Park Service: Johnstown Flood National Memorial**
The Johnstown, Pennsylvania, flood of 1889 was one of the greatest natural disasters in the history of the United States. Here you will learn about the town, the flood, and its victims.

Link to this Internet site from http://www.myreportlinks.com

▶**National Park Service: Valley Forge National Historical Park**
George Washington chose Valley Forge, Pennsylvania, as the winter encampment for his troops in 1777–78. This National Park Service site contains an interactive map of the camp as well as information about the soldiers who persevered through a harsh winter there.

Link to this Internet site from http://www.myreportlinks.com

▶**Pennsylvania Governors Past to Present**
On this site from the Pennsylvania Historical and Museum Commission, you can read biographies of the former governors of Pennsylvania.

Link to this Internet site from http://www.myreportlinks.com

▶**Phila.gov: city @ your service**
The official site of the city of Philadelphia contains city facts, news, government information, and much more. A number of interesting special features can also be found here.

Link to this Internet site from http://www.myreportlinks.com

▶**PBS: Benjamin Franklin**
Ben Franklin, who spent most of his life in Pennsylvania, was a statesman, scientist, printer, inventor, writer, publisher, philosopher, and ambassador. This PBS site contains a wealth of information about his prolific life and work.

Link to this Internet site from http://www.myreportlinks.com

▶**Religious Movements: The Amish**
The Amish are a religious community who came to America from Germany and Switzerland in the eighteenth century. The largest Amish community in the world is in Pennsylvania. Here you will learn about the group's history and beliefs.

Link to this Internet site from http://www.myreportlinks.com

 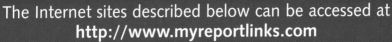
Report Links

The Internet sites described below can be accessed at
http://www.myreportlinks.com

▶**Religious Movements: Quakers**
Pennsylvania was founded as a result of William Penn's pursuit of a
safe haven for Quakers in America. Here you will learn about Quaker
history, current status, and beliefs.

Link to this Internet site from http://www.myreportlinks.com

▶**The Richest Man in the World: Andrew Carnegie**
Andrew Carnegie rose from a poor childhood in Scotland and
Pittsburgh to become one of the richest men in the world by helping
to found the American steel industry. This site profiles Carnegie's life
and his later philanthropy.

Link to this Internet site from http://www.myreportlinks.com

▶**The State Museum of Pennsylvania**
Here at the official site of the State Museum of Pennsylvania you will
learn about a variety of permanent and temporary exhibits, visitor
information, and more.

Link to this Internet site from http://www.myreportlinks.com

▶**USHistory.org: The Liberty Bell**
The Liberty Bell was built to commemorate the fifty-year anniversary of
William Penn's 1701 Charter of Privileges. When it rang to announce
the signing of the Declaration of Independence, it took on a new
significance. This site offers the bell's history, a time line, and more.

Link to this Internet site from http://www.myreportlinks.com

▶**Visiting Independence National Historical Park**
Independence National Historical Park in Philadelphia is the site of the
Liberty Bell, Independence Hall, Congress Hall, and a number of other
buildings of historical significance. This National Park Service site
discusses the history and importance of the park.

Link to this Internet site from http://www.myreportlinks.com

▶**William Penn: Visionary Proprietor**
William Penn was the founder of Pennsylvania. Here you will learn
about his life, his relationship with American Indians, his planning of
the city of Philadelphia, and more. A comprehensive list of William
Penn resources is also included.

Link to this Internet site from http://www.myreportlinks.com

Pennsylvania Facts

▶ **Capital**
Harrisburg

▶ **Gained Statehood**
December 12, 1787, the second
state of the Union

▶ **Population**
12,281,054*

▶ **Animal**
White-tailed deer

▶ **Beverage**
Milk

▶ **Bird**
Ruffed grouse

▶ **Dog**
Great Dane

▶ **Fish**
Brook trout

▶ **Tree**
Eastern hemlock

▶ **Fossil**
Phacops rana (a form of trilo-
bite, an extinct organism related
to crabs and spiders)

▶ **Insect**
Firefly

▶ **Flag**
Approved in 1907, the flag
features the state's coat of arms
on a blue field. Black horses are
on either side of the coat of
arms, with an eagle on top sym-
bolizing the state's sovereignty.
A scroll at the bottom carries
the state motto: "Virtue,
Liberty, and Independence."

▶ **Flower**
Mountain laurel

▶ **Motto**
"Virtue, Liberty,
and Independence"

▶ **Nickname**
The Keystone State

▶ **Song**
"Pennsylvania" was written and
composed by Eddie Khoury
and Ronnie Bonner and
adopted by the state general
assembly in 1990.

Population reflects the 2000 census.

Chapter 1 ▶

Pennsylvania: Birthplace of Freedom

Although Pennsylvania is often thought of as the birthplace of American independence, the state could also be considered a birthplace of religious freedom. In the 1600s, the Quaker belief that no church or priest is needed to be in touch with God outraged many people. ("Quakers" is the more common name for adherents of the Religious Society

Viewing a Document Photo - Microsoft Internet Explorer

File   Edit   View   Favorites   Tools   Help   Links »

.ddress http://www.docheritage.state.pa.us/pics/view.asp?id=1   Go

Done   Internet

▲ William Penn obtained this charter in 1681 from King Charles II of England for a tract of land in America that would come to be known as Pennsylvania.

of Friends.) William Penn, who had been jailed for his Quaker beliefs in England, became involved in a plan to create a safe place for Quakers in the New World. On March 4, 1681, in payment for a debt owed to Penn's father, King Charles II gave Penn a charter to create a colony in the hilly woodlands north of Maryland. The king named the colony *Pennsylvania*—"Penn" for William's father, and "sylvania" after the word "sylvan," which means "wooded or forested."

The Keystone State

With a land area of 44,817 square miles, Pennsylvania is thirty-third in area among the fifty states. It is bordered by the states of New York, New Jersey, Delaware, Maryland, West Virginia, and Ohio, as well as Lake Erie on the state's northwest corner. Shaped like a rectangle, Pennsylvania is 310 miles east to west, and 180 miles north to south.

According to its state constitution, Pennsylvania is a commonwealth—a special designation used by only three other states: Kentucky, Massachusetts, and Virginia. Pennsylvania's nickname, the Keystone State, originally referred to Pennsylvania's central location among the thirteen colonies. Modern Pennsylvanians like to say it refers to the state's key position in the economic and political development of the United States.

Powerful Pennsylvanians

Pennsylvanians have made their marks in many different fields. The most important American document, the Declaration of Independence, was edited and signed by Benjamin Franklin. Although he was born in Boston, Franklin made his life in Philadelphia, working as a writer, printer, and inventor. Franklin was a delegate to the

James Buchanan, the fifteenth president of the United States, was born in a log cabin in Cove Gap, Pennsylvania, a few miles from Mercersburg.

Continental Congress, and he traveled widely to raise support for independence.

The nation's fifteenth president, James Buchanan, was born near Mercersburg and studied law in Lancaster. Later he served in Congress and as a diplomat. He was president from 1857 to 1861. Although he opposed slavery, he felt that the federal government could not force the Southern states to stay in the Union. Buchanan remains the only U.S. president to hail from Pennsylvania.

Giants of Pennsylvania industry included steel kings Andrew Carnegie, Charles Schwab, and J. Pierpont Morgan. Milton Hershey built a successful candy business in Lancaster, and Henry J. Heinz started a food corporation in Pittsburgh that became famous for its ketchup. Many businesses have followed Heinz's famous motto: "To do a common thing uncommonly well brings success."[1]

Other Famous Residents

Aside from politics and industry, Pennsylvania has also produced famous writers, entertainers, scientists, and artists. Writer and marine biologist Rachel Carson published *Silent Spring* in 1962, which many say led to

the modern environmental movement. John Updike published a famous 1961 novel, *Rabbit Run*, that was set in Pennsylvania. Entertainers that were born or lived in the state include Gene Kelly, a dancer and singer known for *Singin' in the Rain*, and Bill Cosby, the comedian and television veteran who created *The Cosby Show.* Other notable Pennsylvanians include anthropologist Margaret Mead and artist Andrew Wyeth.

▶ Natural Wonders

Pennsylvania's natural beauty includes mountain ridges, sweeping valleys, roaring rivers, and country plains. In the Allegheny National Forest, hikers can walk past hillsides covered with rhododendron and mountain laurel. To the northwest, a seven-mile peninsula juts into Lake Erie, with sandy beaches and dunes. Farther east, the Pocono Mountains feature ski resorts, and the dramatic Delaware Water Gap National Recreation Area, which extends into New Jersey, offers hiking, biking, boating, and other forms of recreation.

Far different, but just as beautiful, is architect Frank Lloyd Wright's masterpiece, Fallingwater. Designed in 1935 as a private residence sixty miles southeast of Pittsburgh, Fallingwater is a well-known example of architecture blending with its environment. The building, recently renovated and open to the public, seems to balance on the surrounding rocks and waterfalls.

▶ Historic Hallmarks

Pennsylvania's historic sites are among the most visited in the nation. In Philadelphia, visitors can see the cracked Liberty Bell, which rang to announce the first reading of the Declaration of Independence, and Independence Hall,

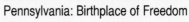
where both the Declaration and the U.S. Constitution were adopted. At Valley Forge National Historical Park, families can see the cabins where George Washington and his army spent the brutally cold winter of 1777–78.

At Gettysburg National Military Park, history buffs can walk along the fields where General Robert E. Lee's army suffered a crushing defeat at the hands of the Union army. And for more lighthearted fun, families can visit HersheyPark, a theme park located in the factory town made famous by Milton Hershey.

▲ *Independence Hall in Philadelphia is one of the most widely visited historical sites in the City of Brotherly Love.*

Chapter 2 ▶

Ridges and Valleys: Land and Climate

Pennsylvania has been shaped by powerful natural forces. The Appalachian Mountains form dramatic ridges and valleys in the eastern part of the state. Scenic rivers wind past the state's most important cities. The highest point in Pennsylvania is Mount Davis in southwestern Somerset County, at 3,213 feet. The lowest point is at sea level, where the Delaware River passes Philadelphia.

▶ Up in the Mountains

The section of the Appalachian Mountains that runs through eastern and south-central Pennsylvania is called the Ridge and Valley Province. These sharp-crested ridges line up one after another like soldiers. The average height of the mountains is between 800 and 1,000 feet. A major part of the Ridge and Valley Province is the Great Valley, which stretches from New York to Georgia. Virginia's portion is the famous Shenandoah Valley. In Pennsylvania, the Great Valley has three names: the Cumberland Valley, the Lebanon Valley, and the Lehigh Valley. The Appalachian Trail, popular with hikers, runs through these mountains as well.

The northern and western parts of the state are dominated by the Allegheny Plateau. A plateau is an elevated, fairly level expanse of land. Yet the Allegheny Plateau is far from flat and boring. It is marked by many cascading streams, rocky terrain, and thick forests.

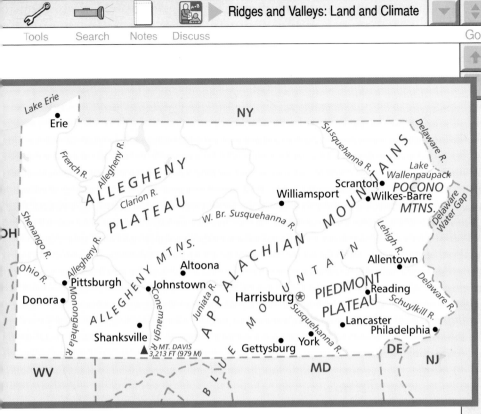

▲ *A map of Pennsylvania.*

▶ Down by the Rivers

As mighty as Pennsylvania's mountains are, the state also boasts several impressive rivers. The 444-mile Susquehanna River curves through eastern Pennsylvania and down to the Chesapeake Bay in Maryland, crossing through the state's anthracite coal region.

The Susquehanna's eastern rival is the Delaware River, which forms the border between Pennsylvania and New Jersey and New York. Near Stroudsburg, the river cuts a scenic gorge, known as the Delaware Water Gap, through Kittatinny Mountain. The river widens as it meets the Schuylkill River near Philadelphia.

Farther west, at Pittsburgh, the Allegheny and the Monongahela rivers come together to form the Ohio

River, which flows west all the way to the Mississippi River. Until 2001, the Pittsburgh Steelers football team played in Three Rivers Stadium, named for the meeting of these famous rivers.

▶ Important Cities

Philadelphia, Pittsburgh, and Harrisburg are three of the state's most important cities. Anchoring the southeast corner of the state, Philadelphia contains many historic sites. These include Independence Hall and the Liberty Bell; Congress Hall, where George Washington gave his last address as president; and Carpenters' Hall, where the First Continental Congress met. According to legend, the Betsy Ross House is where the first American flag was made. Today, Philadelphia is the fifth-largest city in the United

▲ *The Pittsburgh skyline at sunset. In the foreground is the Point, or Point State Park, named for the point where the Ohio, Monongahela, and Allegheny rivers meet.*

States. The "City of Brotherly Love" remains a bustling center for manufacturing and commerce.

In the western part of the state lies Pittsburgh, an industrial powerhouse. Because of its roots in the steel industry, Pittsburgh is often called "Steel City." In modern times, however, Pittsburgh's industries have expanded to include oil refining, printing, and computer technology, among others.

Although much smaller than Pittsburgh and Philadelphia, Harrisburg serves an important purpose: It is Pennsylvania's state capital. Located on the Susquehanna River, Harrisburg is an important inland transportation center. The striking state capitol building has a 272-foot dome modeled after St. Peter's Basilica in Rome, Italy. Nearby museums include the Pennsylvania State Museum, the William Penn Memorial Museum, and the National Civil War Museum. The large Three Mile Island nuclear facility sits ten miles to the south, the site of a 1979 nuclear accident that released harmful radioactive gas into the surrounding environment.

▶ Seasonal Changes

Like most states in the mid-Atlantic region, Pennsylvania enjoys all four seasons. As one moves from the city to the mountainous regions, temperatures generally become cooler, and more precipitation tends to fall. Spring temperatures average around 50°F. In the summer, temperatures can be hot and humid, reaching the 80s. Mild autumns have average high temperatures in the 60s. Winters are cold in Pennsylvania, especially in the northern sections and in the mountains, which usually get several feet of snow a year. Average winter temperatures range from the 20s to the 40s.

▲ *Autumn is especially vibrant in the wooded and rural places of Pennsylvania, such as Lake Naomi, in Monroe County.*

The highest recorded temperature in Pennsylvania, 111°F, occurred on July 10, 1936, in the town of Phoenixville. On the state's coldest day, January 5, 1904, thermometers in the town of Smethport registered −42°F. In 2001, the lakefront city of Erie received 145 inches of snow, setting a new record.

▶ Protecting Animals and Habitat

Although Pennsylvania's forests and rivers provide shelter for many plants and animals, the state's industrial practices and growing cities have destroyed wetlands, forests, grasslands, and other important habitats. Pennsylvania's threatened and endangered animals include the bald eagle, the northern bog turtle, and the Indiana bat. Threatened plants include small whorled pogonia, a type of orchid with yellow-green flowers.

Chapter 3

The Strength of Steel: Economy

No industry has had a greater impact on Pennsylvania's economy than steel.

The steel industry processes mined iron ore into steel and then turns that metal into finished or partially finished products. In the 1880s, largely because of the leadership of steel titans Andrew Carnegie and Charles M. Schwab, the United States was the world's largest producer of the metal. By 1901, Carnegie had sold his Carnegie Steel Company to J. P. Morgan's corporation, U. S. Steel. Three years later, Schwab, who had been president of Carnegie's corporation, bought Bethlehem Steel.

Over the twentieth century, however, the Pennsylvania steel industry declined. Although the industry is sustained by automobile manufacturing and other goods, competition from foreign suppliers has caused Pennsylvania steel to suffer. Between 1998 and 2002, more than fifty thousand steelworker jobs were lost. The once-mighty Bethlehem Steel filed for bankruptcy in 2001, although it is still operating. The industry has supported the establishment of a tariff, or tax, on imported steel. Despite the crisis, in 1997 the steel industry produced shipments worth $8.5 billion.

▶ Coal and Oil

Steel production was itself built on the shoulders of the coal-mining industry, which began in Pennsylvania in the 1700s. Pennsylvania is now the fourth-largest coal producer in the United States, following Kentucky, West Virginia, and Wyoming. Pennsylvania produces two kinds

of coal—anthracite, which is hard coal, and bituminous, which is a softer coal. In 1997, there were 291 coal-mining businesses in the state, providing jobs for more than ten thousand people. Each year, mining contributes about $1.5 billion in direct coal sales and tax revenues of more than $1.5 million to the Pennsylvania economy.

The coal industry has taken a heavy human and environmental toll, however. Since 1870, Pennsylvania has recorded more than fifty-one thousand deaths from mining accidents. And acid drainage from old mines has polluted many Pennsylvania waterways. Today, modern mining methods have improved worker safety, and the state is working to protect streams from the effects of mining.

▲ *A steelworker in one of Pennsylvania's mills. The steel industry in America had its beginnings in Pennsylvania. Steel is still an important part of the state's economy.*

Tools   Search   Notes   Discuss   Go!

In 1859, the world's first commercial oil well was drilled in Titusville, beginning the state's long dependence on the petroleum industry. For decades, Pennsylvania was the nation's top producer of crude oil, until the oil reserves of Texas were tapped at the turn of the century. Pennsylvania is still a leader in oil refining, shipping more than $7.4 billion worth of oil products in 1996.

Farming and Food Processing

In 2001, Pennsylvania had about fifty-nine thousand farms, occupying about 7.7 million acres. Pennsylvania's main crops are mushrooms, wheat and other grains, potatoes, and fruits such as apples and cherries. The state leads the nation in mushroom production, producing about 443 billion pounds per year. Yet the vast majority of the state's farm income—69 percent—comes from the sale of livestock and livestock products. The state produced 6.7 percent of the nation's total supply of milk in 2000.

Pennsylvania is also famous for its food production. The three *H*'s of the state's food industry are Heinz, Hershey, and Hanover. Although the H. J. Heinz Company remains famous for its "57 Varieties" of ketchup and other condiments, the company now has a diverse line of foods and offices worldwide. In 2001, the Pittsburgh Steelers' new stadium was named Heinz Field after the historic company. That same year, the Hershey Foods Corporation's net sales were $4.1 billion. And the town of Hanover is the headquarters of well-known snack-food companies, including Snyder's of Hanover, best known for its pretzels, and Utz Quality Foods, which manufactures potato chips and other snacks.

▲ *The Drake Well Museum in Titusville commemorates the place where Edwin Drake drilled the world's first successful oil well, on August 27, 1859. Drake's accomplishment signified the birth of the modern petroleum industry.*

▶ Tourism

Whether visitors hike in the mountains, play a round of golf, or paddle in a river, tourism plays a major part in Pennsylvania's economy. In 1999, the tourism industry supported more than 531,605 jobs. Direct and indirect spending by travelers totaled $26 billion that year.

Sports are big business in Pennsylvania as well. Golfing and related activities bring in about $2.3 billion to the Pennsylvania economy each year. Professional sports teams include the Pittsburgh Steelers, Pirates, and Penguins, and the Philadelphia Eagles, Phillies, 76ers, and Flyers. The sports teams of Pennsylvania State University are beloved statewide as well.

▶ Transportation

Historically, the backbone of Pennsylvania industry and transportation has been its railroad system. The state's growing railroad system was first put to widespread use during the Civil War. After the war, advances in steel manufacturing led to explosive growth in the railroad network, which expanded from four thousand miles of track in 1870 to more than ten thousand miles in 1900. Today, Amtrak lines crisscross the state, with most routes passing through Philadelphia.

The state's largest airports are found in Philadelphia, Pittsburgh, and Harrisburg. The state also maintains a broad network of interstate and state highways and roads. Perhaps the most famous of these roads is the Pennsylvania Turnpike, which runs roughly east to west for 531 miles. The toll road is an important source of state income, bringing in nearly $376 million in fiscal year 2001.

Waterways are still widely used for moving goods to such ports as Philadelphia, Pittsburgh, and Erie. Erie is located on the Great Lakes St. Lawrence Seaway, which extends for more than two thousand nautical miles from the Atlantic Ocean to Lake Superior.

▶ Communication and Technology

Ever since Benjamin Franklin published the *Pennsylvania Gazette* in 1728, publishing has been a major business in Pennsylvania. The first American daily newspaper, the *Pennsylvania Packet and General Advertiser*, was published in Philadelphia in 1784. Two years later, the *Pittsburgh Post-Gazette* was founded, the first newspaper west of the Allegheny Mountains. Today, the *Post-Gazette*'s daily circulation is more than 243,000. The *Philadelphia Inquirer* was

first published in 1829 and now has a daily circulation of about 344,000. The *Pittsburgh Courier*, founded in 1907, was one of the nation's leading African-American newspapers for many decades. It is now published under the name *The New Pittsburgh Courier*.

Pennsylvania also has about thirty-five major network television stations and nearly five hundred radio stations. Philadelphia is considered the fourth-largest radio market in the United States.

As for technology, the American Electronics Association announced in its 2002 annual *Cyberstates* report that Pennsylvania had added 1,300 tech jobs in 2001, for a total of 194,000 statewide. The state ranks third in the nation in consumer electronics manufacturing and fifth in industrial electronics and electronic components.

▲ *PNC Park, which opened in 2001, is home to the National League's Pittsburgh Pirates. The new stadium is the second-smallest Major League ballpark, built to recapture the more intimate feel of ballparks of the past.*

Chapter 4 ▶

Building Better Lives: Government

The American two-chamber political system is as old as the colonies themselves. Such a system, known as a bicameral legislature, allows for checks and balances so that no one group or political party can make all the decisions. Yet in 1701, Pennsylvania founded the only unicameral legislature in all the British colonies. The one-chamber assembly could consider legislation, elect officers, appoint committees, and decide the length of the legislative session. The system continued until 1790, when a new constitution established the state's current bicameral legislature.

William Penn supported keeping the court system as simple as possible. He stated that "all pleadings, processes, and records in courts, shall be short, and in English, and in an ordinary and plain character, that they may be understood, and justice speedily administered."[1] Today, the state's court cases may not always be short and speedy, but the judicial branch remains streamlined and effective.

▶ The Legislative Branch

The Pennsylvania state legislature is known as the general assembly, which consists of a 50-member senate and a 203-member house of representatives. Members of the senate serve four-year terms, while house members serve two-year terms. Legislative sessions last for one calendar year. To be elected, state senators must be at least twenty-five years old and representatives at least twenty-one years old. They must be citizens and inhabitants of the state

▲ The Pennsylvania State Capitol, in Harrisburg, is the home of the Pennsylvania General Assembly, the state's lawmaking body.

for four years and have lived in their elected districts for one year.

Pennsylvania ratified new constitutions in 1776, 1790, 1838, and 1874. Several new proposals were added to the state constitution in 1968. One of these allows a governor to serve two consecutive terms of four years each. Previously, the governor was not allowed to serve two terms in a row.

In the U.S. Congress, Pennsylvania is represented by two senators and twenty-one representatives. The state has twenty-three votes in the Electoral College.

▶ The Executive Branch

According to the Pennsylvania Constitution, the governor and lieutenant governor must be citizens of the United States and at least thirty years old. In addition, they must have lived in the commonwealth for at least seven years before the election. The youngest governor was Robert Pattison, who was thirty-two when he was elected to two

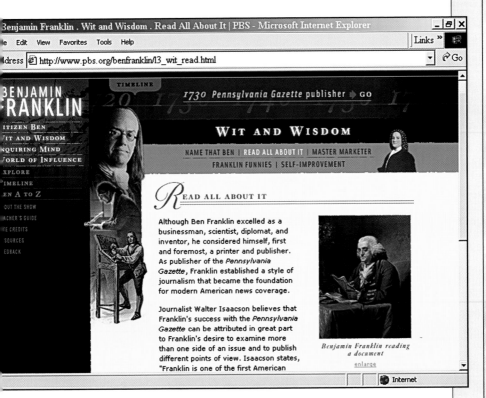

Benjamin Franklin . Wit and Wisdom . Read All About It | PBS - Microsoft Internet Explorer

File   Edit   View   Favorites   Tools   Help   Links »

Address http://www.pbs.org/benfranklin/13_wit_read.html   Go

BENJAMIN FRANKLIN

CITIZEN BEN
WIT AND WISDOM
INQUIRING MIND
WORLD OF INFLUENCE
EXPLORE
TIMELINE
BEN A TO Z
ABOUT THE SHOW
TEACHER'S GUIDE
THE CREDITS
SOURCES
FEEDBACK

TIMELINE   1730 Pennsylvania Gazette publisher ▶ GO

WIT AND WISDOM

NAME THAT BEN | READ ALL ABOUT IT | MASTER MARKETER
FRANKLIN FUNNIES | SELF-IMPROVEMENT

READ ALL ABOUT IT

Although Ben Franklin excelled as a businessman, scientist, diplomat, and inventor, he considered himself, first and foremost, a printer and publisher. As publisher of the *Pennsylvania Gazette*, Franklin established a style of journalism that became the foundation for modern American news coverage.

Journalist Walter Isaacson believes that Franklin's success with the *Pennsylvania Gazette* can be attributed in great part to Franklin's desire to examine more than one side of an issue and to publish different points of view. Isaacson states, "Franklin is one of the first American

Benjamin Franklin reading a document
enlarge

🌐 Internet

▲ At age seventeen, Ben Franklin left Boston for Philadelphia. At age eighty-four, he died there. In the interim, he lived for a time in London and Paris, but Philadelphia was the home of the famous philosopher, statesman, printer, scientist, and Founding Father.

terms in the late 1800s. In 1959, when elected, David Lawrence became Pennsylvania's oldest governor at age sixty-nine.

Pennsylvania's governors have included some of the nation's most influential people. Following the American Revolution, Benjamin Franklin served one term as president of the Supreme Executive Council, as the government was called then. During the Civil War, Governor Andrew Gregg Curtin provided advice and support to President Lincoln. Notable twentieth-century governors include Gifford Pinchot, who served two terms, from 1923 to 1927 and from 1931 to 1935. A forester by profession, Pinchot was the founding director of the United States Forest Service. He had also helped Theodore Roosevelt found the Progressive Party in 1912. As governor, Pinchot supported state and national conservation efforts.

▶ The Judicial Branch

Pennsylvania has a unified judicial system, which means that all courts fall under the supervision of the state supreme court. Below the high court are the two appellate courts, the superior court and the commonwealth court, followed by the courts of common pleas. Below that is a wide network of community courts, traffic courts, and police courts.

Seven justices serve on the state supreme court, including one chief justice, an honor given to the longest-serving justice. Justices are elected by the voters to a term of ten years. After ten years, they can choose to be placed back on the ballot for retention, or they can step down. If vacancies occur, the governor can select someone to fill the position.

Chapter 5 ▶

Spirit of Independence: History

When William Penn arrived in his new colony in 1682, he quickly developed policies for a colonial government and supervised plans for the new city of Philadelphia. Penn treated the local American Indian tribes with respect. He drafted an agreement with the Delaware tribe, for example, saying that "no man shall by any ways or means in word or deed affront or wrong any Indians. . . ."[1]

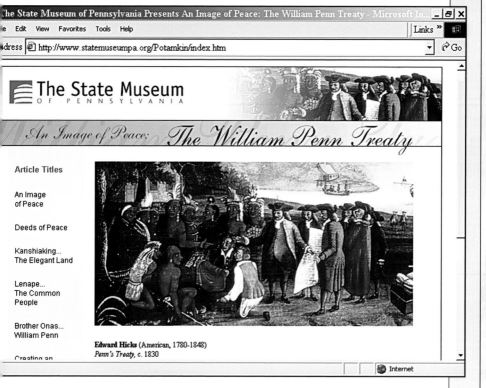

▲ William Penn's treaty with the Delaware or Lenni Lenape tribe is captured in this early American painting by Edward Hicks, who was, like Penn, a Quaker.

The Susquehannock and the Shawnee, as well as many tribes smaller in number, also lived in Pennsylvania. Hoping to prevent conflict, Penn and his successors were careful to purchase the Indians' claims to the land. But relations with American Indians worsened. The French and Indian War (1754–63) engaged British, French, and American Indian forces in a fight for territory near present-day Pittsburgh. Eventually, the British won, allowing the colonies to expand, but Indian tribes began to leave Pennsylvania and head west as colonial settlement increased.

▶ The Quaker Influence

Penn's Quaker faith had a deep effect on the growing colony. Quakers favored peaceful negotiations over warfare, and they focused on education and charity work. They also opposed the practice of slavery, which existed in other colonies. By 1790, ten thousand slaves had been brought to Pennsylvania. However, the Pennsylvania Gradual Abolition Act of 1780 meant that slavery would eventually be phased out. This was the first law that abolished, or ended, slavery in the United States.

▶ The Pennsylvania Dutch

The religious freedom enjoyed by the Quakers brought other immigrants to Pennsylvania throughout the eighteenth century. "When I came into this province and found everything to the contrary [of] where I came from," wrote a German immigrant, "I wrote largely to all my friends and acquaintances of the civil and religious liberties [and] privileges, and of all the goodness I have heard and seen."[2]

The Germans, Dutch, and Swiss who settled in Pennsylvania in the early eighteenth century became known collectively as the Pennsylvania Dutch, and many of them belonged to religious groups that had been persecuted in their homelands. One of those groups, the old order Amish, separated from the larger Mennonite church and settled in southeastern Pennsylvania in rich farming areas.

The Revolutionary War

Although the American colonists enjoyed religious freedoms, they disagreed with many British colonial policies. To express their views, the colonies sent delegates to the First Continental Congress, held in Carpenters' Hall, Philadelphia, from September 5 to October 26, 1774. After the Second Continental Congress, held in May 1775, support for independence was strong. That spring, fighting at Lexington and Concord, Massachusetts, began the American Revolution, and George Washington

▲ *Carpenters' Hall in Philadelphia has been the home or meeting place of many historic American institutions, including the First Continental Congress, Benjamin Franklin's library company, and the First and Second Banks of the United States.*

became commander in chief. The following year, Virginian Thomas Jefferson was asked to write a draft of the Declaration of Independence, which was revised by Benjamin Franklin. The declaration was adopted on July 4, 1776. That fall, the commonwealth's first constitution, including a Declaration of Rights, was adopted as well.

But the war dragged on. After a bitter defeat that left Philadelphia in British control, Washington's army was forced to spend the winter of 1777–78 at Valley Forge, twenty miles northwest of Philadelphia. This was the low point for the battered Continental Army, which lacked food and supplies. One in ten men died, nearly all from disease. "We have frequently suffered temporary want and great inconveniences," Washington wrote, "and for several days past, we have experienced little less than a famine in camp. . . ."[3]

Despite the hardships, the army prepared for war. Under the leadership of General Friedrich Wilhelm von Steuben, a former Prussian army officer, soldiers were trained to line up, march, and rapidly load and fire their muskets. By the following summer, Washington was able to lead the army to many victories, ending with the British surrender at Yorktown, Virginia, in 1781.

A constitution for the new nation was developed at the first Constitutional Convention, which met in Philadelphia in May 1787. The Pennsylvania Assembly sent eight delegates to the convention, including Ben Franklin. Pennsylvania's delegation signed the finished United States Constitution on September 17 and ratified, or approved, it on December 12, 1787.

Philadelphia served as the capital of the young nation from 1790 to 1800, when the capital was moved to Washington, D.C.

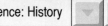

▲ *While the British occupied nearby Philadelphia, the Continental Army spent the winter of 1777–78 at Valley Forge and, under extremely harsh conditions, became a much better prepared military force.*

▶ The Slavery Issue

In the nineteenth century, the practice of slavery had become a divisive issue. People in Northern states pushed for the abolition of slavery, but Southern states defended the practice. Whenever new states were added to the nation, often called the Union, debates arose over whether slavery should be allowed there. Women were actively involved in the abolition movement, and this was the case in Pennsylvania. In 1833, Lucretia Mott organized the Philadelphia Female Anti-Slavery Society.

But not all Pennsylvanians were against slavery or for equality among the races, as witnessed by the state's 1838 constitution, which took away the voting rights of African

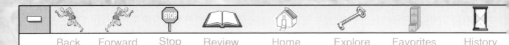

◀ *After gaining freedom in Pennsylvania, Harriet Tubman continued to travel into Maryland to help other African Americans escape slavery.*

Americans. As a Northern state whose southern border touched Maryland, a slaveholding state, Pennsylvania was directly affected by the Fugitive Slave Law of 1850. That law made it illegal for people to help African Americans who had escaped slavery. Yet, with its large Quaker population, which believed slavery was immoral, Pennsylvania became a haven for African Americans escaping slavery through the Underground Railroad, a network of people and safe houses. Harriet Tubman, a former slave who was led from Maryland to freedom in Pennsylvania by Quaker abolitionists, became one of the railroad's greatest "conductors." For at least ten years, she made trips back into Maryland to lead other African Americans to freedom in the North.

By December 1860, tensions over slavery exploded when South Carolina seceded, or withdrew, from the Union. By the following spring, ten other Southern states had joined South Carolina to create the Confederate States of America. Until then, the Mason-Dixon line, which forms Pennsylvania's southern border, was accepted as the unofficial boundary between North and South. Yet Maryland, below this boundary, chose to stay in the Union.

The Civil War

In April 1861, the first shots of the Civil War were fired at Fort Sumter, South Carolina. President Abraham Lincoln soon called for troops to fight the Confederates. Five Pennsylvania militia companies were the first to respond. By war's end about 350,000 Pennsylvanians—including 8,600 African-American volunteers—would serve. Pennsylvania also sent several officers to the war, including George Gordon Meade, John F. Reynolds, George B. McClellan, and Winfield Scott Hancock.

Pennsylvania's iron and textile industries were put to work supplying the Union army. Gun factories in Philadelphia and Reading produced rifles and ammunition. The Philadelphia Navy Yard built gunboats. And Pennsylvania's well-developed railroad system moved supplies to troops stationed to the south.

War Moves North

Although most of the Civil War was fought in the South, the war's most famous battle took place July 1–3, 1863, in Gettysburg, a small railroad hub in south-central Pennsylvania. The Confederate army, led by General Robert E. Lee, had enjoyed a string of victories in the South. Lee was confident that he could push north, cutting off Union supply lines and threatening the nation's capital. Hearing rumors of Lee's movements, President Lincoln asked Pennsylvanian George Meade to lead the Union army.

When the Confederates reached Gettysburg, Meade's men were ready. The Union soldiers were stretched along

http://www.nps.gov/gett/gettcyclo.jpg - Microsoft Internet Explorer

File　Edit　View　Favorites　Tools　Help

Address　http://www.nps.gov/gett/gettcyclo.jpg

Done　　Internet

▲ *This oil painting titled* Pickett's Charge *depicts the pivotal moment of the Battle of Gettysburg, which was the final failed Confederate assault on July 3, 1863.*

a low ridge, where they pushed back the attacking Confederate army. At the end of the three-day battle, the Union army had held their position, and Lee's army had retreated. But the battle caused more than 51,000 casualties—the most of any battle of the Civil War. That November, President Lincoln attended the dedication of a new national cemetery at Gettysburg. There, in what would come to be known as the Gettysburg Address, Lincoln gave a brief but compelling speech to honor the sacrifice of the soldiers who had died there.

In July 1864, Confederate raiders invaded the town of Chambersburg, twenty-five miles west of Gettysburg, and burned it to the ground. Two thirds of the townspeople were left homeless. The state later paid citizens more than $1.6 million to make up for their losses.

Steel and Strikes

By the mid-nineteenth century, steel had become Pennsylvania's main industry, dependent on the mining of iron ore and coal. The industry was largely built by Andrew Carnegie, a Scottish immigrant who wanted to develop steel to make stronger railroad tracks. In 1875 he opened the Edgar Thomson Steel Works, primarily to serve the Pennsylvania Railroad. But by the 1890s, everything from the tallest skyscraper to the smallest soup can was made from steel, and Carnegie had become a rich man.

▲ Coal mining, long part of Pennsylvania's economy, was a dangerous and dirty job, and children were often employed in mining work. These "boy laborers" are pictured in 1911 outside the Ewen Breaker, a plant that processed coal in South Pittstown.

Not everyone who worked in steel became wealthy, however. In fact, the steel and coal industries depended on the cheap labor provided by European immigrants. Most worked twelve hours a day, seven days a week. In the decade after the Civil War, miners began to protest their unhealthy and dangerous working and living conditions. A group of chiefly Irish-American coal miners from Pennsylvania's anthracite mines, who became known as the Molly Maguires, staged attacks against the industry bosses. The Mollies, as they were called, had protested their extremely low wages and horrible working conditions, but their cries were not heeded. Some Mollies were later hanged for committing murder, although there is now evidence that they were not guilty of those crimes.

By the end of the century, steel laborers had organized a union called the Amalgamated Association of Iron and Steel Workers. On June 29, 1892, union workers organized a strike against the Carnegie Steel Company in Homestead, Pennsylvania, to protest a proposed wage cut. In response, the company's general manager, Henry C. Frick, hired hundreds of detectives to protect the plant. A battle broke out, and several men were injured or killed. After that, the union movement was weakened for decades.

▶ The Johnstown Flood

Even with the labor strikes, many Pennsylvania cities and towns thrived on successful mining and steel operations. This was true in the city of Johnstown, located in western Pennsylvania. In 1889, with a population of thirty thousand, Johnstown was a bustling city. But disaster loomed above the town.

About fourteen miles upstream on the Little Conemaugh River, the three-mile-long Lake Conemaugh

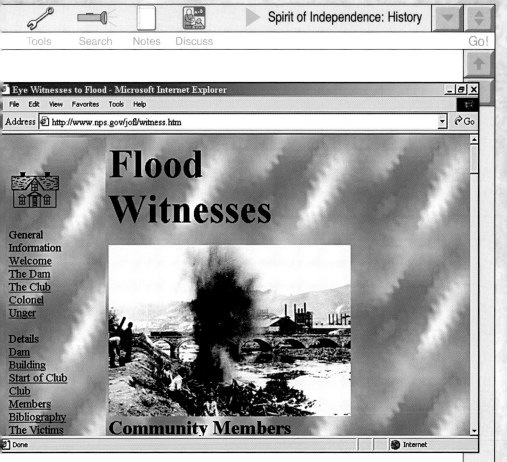

Eye Witnesses to Flood - Microsoft Internet Explorer

File   Edit   View   Favorites   Tools   Help

Address   http://www.nps.gov/jofl/witness.htm   Go

Flood Witnesses

General Information
Welcome
The Dam
The Club
Colonel Unger

Details
Dam Building
Start of Club
Club Members
Bibliography
The Victims

Community Members

Done   Internet

▲ *The story of the Johnstown Flood was the largest news story of the late nineteenth century in America. More than two thousand people perished on May 31, 1889, when the South Fork Dam broke.*

was held in by the old South Fork Dam. The dam was poorly maintained, threatening to break at any moment. On May 31, 1889, residents heard a low rumble, which grew to a roar like a freight train. After a night of heavy rains, South Fork Dam had broken, sending 20 million tons of water down the narrow valley.

The flood wiped out the valley, sending the towns-people running for higher ground. The Chapman family, for example, ran for their attic as water rushed into their home. "We all stood there in the middle of the floor, waiting our turn to be swept away, and expecting every minute

to be drowned," Mrs. Chapman recalled later.[4] The flood ultimately killed 2,209 people and destroyed miles of property. It would take years for Johnstown to recover.

The Twentieth Century

By the turn of the century, labor unions were gaining power once again. In 1881, the Federation of Organized Trades and Labor Unions was formed during a meeting in Pittsburgh. This group, later renamed the American Federation of Labor (AFL), won higher wages and shorter hours for workers. By the 1930s, a rival group, the Congress of Industrial Organizations (CIO), had formed, winning many members from the steel and automobile industries. In 1955, the two labor unions merged to become the AFL-CIO. This organization, whose roots lie in Pennsylvania industry, now has more than 13 million members.

Battles at Home and Abroad

Pennsylvania's factories were a vital part of American participation in World War I. Nearly three thousand separate companies manufactured war supplies. Pennsylvanians also held high ranks. General Tasker Bliss, a native of Lewisburg, was appointed the army's chief of staff in 1917. He was followed as chief of staff by General Peyton C. March, originally from Easton.

During World War II, more Congressional Medals of Honor were awarded to Pennsylvanians than to citizens of any other state. George C. Marshall, who served as the army's chief of staff, was a native of Uniontown. His plan to aid war-torn Europe, which became known as the Marshall Plan, helped to rebuild the Western European economy. Henry H. Arnold, who directed the army's air forces, was born in Gladwyne. Once again, Pennsylvania's factories

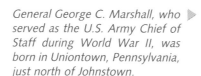

General George C. Marshall, who served as the U.S. Army Chief of Staff during World War II, was born in Uniontown, Pennsylvania, just north of Johnstown.

produced planes, tanks, guns, and ammunition.

After the war, concerns about African-American equality gave rise to the civil rights movement of the 1950s and 1960s. Increasingly, African Americans opposed the practice of segregation, which meant that blacks and whites had to use separate facilities. In Pittsburgh, for example, blacks and whites swam in separate swimming pools. Civil rights organizations filed a lawsuit opposing the policy. By 1953, the city opened pools to all people and began to hire African-American lifeguards.

In 1967, the state convened a Constitutional Convention to revise the 1874 Constitution. Among other changes, a new provision protected the civil rights of all Pennsylvanians.

September 11 and Shanksville

On September 11, 2001, the deadliest terrorist attacks in American history took place. Hijackers crashed airplanes into the two World Trade Center towers in New York City and the Pentagon in Arlington, Virginia, just outside

Washington, D.C., killing more than three thousand people. A fourth hijacked plane, United Flight 93, had taken off from Newark, New Jersey, en route to San Francisco, with forty passengers and crew on board. That plane was being steered toward Washington, D.C., when a group of the passengers decided to take action against their hijackers. The plane crashed in a field near the tiny town of Shanksville, in western Pennsylvania. All aboard were killed, but the actions of those passengers have been hailed as heroic, since it is believed that the intended target would have resulted in the deaths of many more people.

The crash has turned Shanksville into a destination for those who want to remember the victims. In 2002, President George W. Bush signed a law stating that a permanent memorial to the Flight 93 victims would be built in Shanksville.

The September 11 attacks also led to the creation of the new cabinet-level Department of Homeland Security. Tom Ridge, who had served as Pennsylvania governor since 1995, was named the department's first secretary. Ridge visited Shanksville on the one-year anniversary of the crash. "Today, I believe, we also honor a community," he said. "The people of Shanksville and Somerset County embraced the families of Flight 93 as their own. Through kindnesses large and small, they turned strangers into good, good friends."[5]

▶ A Mining Miracle

In July 2002, nine coal miners became trapped in a flooded mine shaft at the Quecreek Mine in Somerset County, not far from Shanksville and only thirty miles from where the massive flood tore through Johnstown a

▲ Miners at the Quecreek Mine are seen here embracing each other after all nine miners who had been trapped were rescued.

century earlier. Above ground, emergency workers found a "super drill" to open a rescue shaft to the men. But the process was slow. For more than three days, the miners kept each other's spirits up, sharing the one sandwich they had. Finally, the shaft reached the miners, and the rescuers were able to hoist the men up to safety, one by one.

The bravery and strength of the miners has been repeated in many other episodes in Pennsylvania's history. Pennsylvanians have built new homes on the frontier, have been instrumental in the nation's independence, have shed their blood to save the Union, and have carved industries out of the ground. Always hardworking and ready to lend a hand, Pennsylvanians are sure to continue this tradition far into the future.

Chapter 1. Pennsylvania: Birthplace of Freedom

1. Heinz Corporation Web site, "About Heinz," n.d., <http://www.heinz.com/jsp/history.jsp> (April 15, 2003).

Chapter 4. Building Better Lives: Government

1. Joseph E. Illick, *Colonial Pennsylvania: A History* (New York: Scribner, 1976), p. 71.

Chapter 5. Spirit of Independence: History

1. Sylvester K. Stevens, *Pennsylvania: Birthplace of a Nation* (New York: Random House, 1964), p. 36.

2. Joseph E. Illick, *Colonial Pennsylvania: A History* (New York: Scribner, 1976), p. 127.

3. George Washington, letter to Patrick Henry, February 19, 1778, *The George Washington Papers at the Library of Congress, 1741–1799,* n.d., <http://memory.loc.gov/ammem/gwhtml/gwhome.html> (April 15, 2003).

4. David G. McCullough, *The Johnstown Flood* (New York: Simon and Schuster, 1968), pp. 154–155.

5. PBS, *NewsHour with Jim Lehrer*, "Shanksville Ceremony" transcript, September 11, 2002, <www.pbs.org/newshour/terrorism/sept11/pa_textridge.html> (May 5, 2003).

Further Reading

Coleman, Bill. *The Gift to Be Simple: Life in the Amish Country.* San Francisco: Chronicle Books, 2001.

Danson, Edwin. *Drawing the Line: How Mason and Dixon Surveyed the Most Famous Border in America.* New York: John Wiley, 2001.

Hylton, Thomas, Blair Seitz, and Mary Warner Denadai. *Save Our Land, Save Our Towns: A Plan for Pennsylvania.* Harrisburg, Pa.: Rb Books, 2000.

Ingram, Scott. *Pennsylvania: The Keystone State.* Milwaukee: Gareth Stevens Incorporated, 2002.

Knight, James E. *The Winter at Valley Forge: Survival and Victory.* Mahwah, N.J.: Troll Communications, LLC, 1999.

Krass, Peter. *Carnegie.* New York: John Wiley & Sons, 2002.

Lilly, Melinda. *Quakers in Early America.* Vero Beach, Fla.: Rourke Publishing, LLC, 2002.

Sherrow, Victoria. *Pennsylvania.* Farmington Hills, Mich.: Lucent Books, 2001.

Thompson, Kathleen. *Pennsylvania.* Austin, Tex.: Raintree Steck-Vaughn Publishers, 1996.

Van Diver, Bradford B. *Roadside Geology of Pennsylvania.* Missoula, Mont.: Mountain Press, 1990.

Wills, Charles A. *A Historical Album of Pennsylvania.* Brookfield, Conn.: Millbrook Press, Inc., 1996.

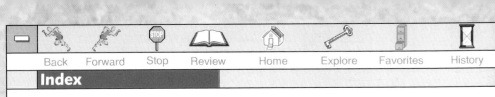